WARNING: Arturo Azurdia's *Connected Christianity* will make people uncomfortable. Whether we are inclined to take refuge in Christian 'bunkers' (insulated from all but superficial contact with the dying people and corroding culture around us) or to blend like chameleons into that very culture (our priorities and pastimes indistinguishable from the environment), Dr. Azurdia's heart-searching study of Jesus' high priestly prayer for us—'I do not ask that you take them out of the world, but that you keep them from the evil one' (John 17:15)—will prick our consciences and challenge us with Christ's call to a mission of holiness that seeks graceful connection with our neighbors and coworkers. Yet because this is Jesus' prayer, sealed by his self-consecration for us on the cross, these meditations do not leave us wallowing in guilt but energized by love for the Savior, eager to engage the world with the gospel of his grace. Despite the warning (or because of it) by all means read this book, slowly and prayerfully.

Dennis E. Johnson
Professor of Practical Theology
Westminster Seminary California
Escondido, California

Christians always need help living in the world while they do not belong to the world. Art Arzudio sought to do this at the Aberystwyth Conference in the following messages. The third address I remember as being particularly helpful. We are sent by God to work right in the midst of this groaning creation day by day. Just as the Father sent his Son into this world so the Son sends us. We go to sinners on the same errand of self-denying love. We don't wait until they come to us on our terms. Jesus says that he doesn't pray that we will be taken out of the world - for we are the salt and light of the world - but he does pray that we will be kept from the evil. Jesus was a friend of sinners and he visited their houses and he spoke to them and dealt with them, trying to help them. What are they engaged in? What are their interests? What burdens do they carry? When do they weep? What gives them joy? You go to learn and you become interested. Some of the things they enthuse about are unworthy. They are not interesting to you, but what of that? You do not stop the flow of kindness towards them. You try to put yourself in their shoes. You look at things from their perspective. Then they begin to have some confidence in you. They discover that you mind the things they mind. You notice and appreciate them. This is living in harmony with people who are not Christians. You do not offer them kindness on your terms but in submission to him who told us to go into all the world

Geoff Thomas,
h, (Independent),
erystwyth, Wales

D0994564

'In the world' but 'not of the world' … this call, command and expectation of our Savior has challenged individual Christians and churches since His Ascension. To accomplish our mission we have to be 'in the world' but it is equally true that we must not be 'of the world'. Therefore, our Lord does not want 'the world' in us. Arturo Azurdia has given us not only the challenge but also a focus and direction as to how to be fully 'in the world' yet intentional not 'of the world'. Many believers and churches, in the name of faithfulness disengage from the world and become museums of religion. Other Christians and churches connect to the world and become just like it. Contextualization without conformity. Being different without disengaging. This book will not only keep the challenge before us but give to us clarity and direction for the Christ-centered and Gospel-driven as well as Holy Spirit-empowered answers from the Word of God. You will want to read this … probably more than once.

Harry L. Reeder, III
Pastor of Preaching and Leadership
Briarwood Presbyterian Church
Birmingham, Alabama

To describe the Christian life as call to a 'holy worldliness' sounds like verbal and spiritual nonsense. In this little book Art Azurdia seeks to persuade us that nothing short of a meaningfully worldly approach can really claim to be authentically Christian. By opening up the words of Jesus in John 17 we are led by the hand to see that holiness and worldly engagement are the outcome of obeying Christ's commission, the consequence of his suffering for his people on the cross, and are sustained by his continuing work as our high priest at God's right hand. If your Christian life is veering off towards a sinful worldliness where you are being shaped in your aspirations by a rebellious world, or towards a sinful reluctance to have any meaningful relationships with non-Christians, this book will steer you back in the right direction.

Martin Downes
Christ Church
Deeside, England

Connected Christianity:

Engaging Culture Without Compromise

Arturo G. Azurdia III

BRYNTIRION PRESS

CHRISTIAN
FOCUS

Unless otherwise indicated all Scripture quotations are taken from *The Holy Bible, English Standard Version* (esv). Copyright © 2001 by Crossway Bibles, a publishing ministry of Good News Publishers. Used by permission. All rights reserved.

Dr. Arturo G. Azurdia III is Associate Professor of Pastoral Theology and Director of Pastoral Mentoring at Western Seminary in Portland, Oregon. He is a native of the San Francisco Bay Area, having attended the California State University at Hayward where he received a B. A. in Music Performance. His M. Div. was earned from The American Baptist Seminary of the West in Berkeley, California, and his D. Min. from Westminster Seminary in Escondido, California. He was the founding minister of Christ Community Church in Fairfield, California, where he subsequently pastored for 19 years.

Art is the author of *Spirit Empowered Preaching* (Christian Focus Publications), and a contributing author in three additional volumes: *Heralds of the King* (Crossway), *The Compromised Church* (Crossway) and *Reforming Pastoral Ministry* (Crossway). He is editor of *The Spurgeon Fellowship Journal* and is a frequent speaker at various national and international conferences. His sermons can be heard online at www.spiritempoweredpreaching.com

Copyright© Arturo Azurdia 2009

ISBN 978-1-84550-468-7

10 9 8 7 6 5 4 3 2 1

Published in 2009
by
Christian Focus Publications Ltd.,
Geanies House, Fearn, Ross-shire,
IV20 1TW, Scotland, Great Britain
with
Bryntirion Press
Pen-y-bont ar Ogwr/Bridgend
CF31 4DX, Wales , Great Britain

www.christianfocus.com

Cover design by Paul Lewis
Printed by Norhaven A/S, Denmark

Contents

Dedication

To my dear brother, Don Doehla ...
a faithful friend,
a fellow elder,
and a worldly Christian *par excellence.*

Acknowledgements

To the Management Board of the Evangelical Movement of Wales ...
Thank you for the invitation to preach at the Aberystwyth conference. It is a high honor that simultaneously begets a deepened humility.

To Philip, Karyn, and Gareth Swann ...
Thank you for the warm hospitality you have extended to me during my visits to Wales. Your home is distinguished by an extraordinary grace and happiness.

To Lori Azurdia ...
You are the unique instrument of God in my life. I will always love you for seeking to make our children authentically Christian *and* meaningfully worldly.

To Melissa Leary ...
If greatness is defined as one who serves, then you are chief among the great. You have often placed me ahead of yourself during this project. Thank you, dear friend.

Preface

From my earliest days of attending church, I can remember our pastor saying nearly every Sunday: 'Churches are like hospitals.' I've given this statement a great deal of thought throughout the years and have come to recognize the truth in it. Churches *are* communities appropriate for sick people. That having been said, no hospital anywhere grants admittance to people plagued with infirmities and then allows them to remain as they are. Such is not a hospital, but a *hospice*. The objective of a *hospital* is to identify the problem, diagnose its source, determine and administer the appropriate remedy, and then watch for transformation. Patients are not allowed to occupy a bed, refuse medication, and then justify their right to remain there. Why not? Because a hospital exists to make people better, not keep them the way they were when admitted.

Is this not also, in large part, the aim of Christian ministry? To make people healthy and strong? Vibrant and vital? Is it not the ambition of the gospel to make people increasingly more Christian? If so, then it must be understood there are certain issues so essential to the ongoing development and health of the Christian life that it is the God-given duty of gospel ministers to speak to them again and again. The subject before us falls precisely into this category. It is one indispensable to spiritual health. To neglect it will forever impede growth into the likeness of Jesus Christ. Consider now these words taken from the great high-priestly prayer of our Lord Jesus – from the chapter described by Martin Luther as 'The Holy of Holies' in all of the Word of God:

> Sanctify them in the truth; your word is truth. As you sent me into the world, so I have sent them into the world. And for their sake I consecrate myself, that they also may be sanctified in truth (John 17:17-19).

1

As you sent me into the world, so I have sent them into the world
(John 17:18).

1

A Worldly Christianity

Ralph Kuyper recounts the story of an eight-year-old girl attending Vacation Bible School at his church. On one particular afternoon she found her way into his study and, to his great surprise, asked: 'Mr. Kuyper, is it all right if I commit suicide?' The young pastor was startled, but he had learned never to respond to a child's question with a quick *yes* or *no* without first discovering the child's reason for the inquiry.

'Mary,' he said, 'why would you ever want to commit suicide?'

'Well,' she answered, 'It's because of what I learned in Bible School this morning.'

'What in the world did she learn in Bible School?' Kuyper thought to himself.

'We were taught that heaven is a wonderful place: no fear, no crying, no fighting. We were taught that

15

when we die, we go to be with Jesus. Did I hear it right, Mr Kuyper?'

'Yes, Mary, you heard it right. But why would you want to commit suicide?'

'Well, you've been to my house. You know my mommy and daddy. They don't know Jesus. They get drunk nearly every night, so we have to get ourselves up in the morning. We have to make our own breakfast and go to school in dirty clothes. The other children make fun of us. And then when we come home again we hear fighting and other things that make us afraid. Why shouldn't I commit suicide? Wouldn't heaven be better?'

That little girl was not dealing with theory – contemplating the theological mysteries of the intermediate state. She was dealing with reality. And it forced her to a question we have all asked from time to time, especially those of us who are Christians: 'Why are we in this world anyway? What's the purpose of it all? *Wouldn't heaven be better?* If this world is truly and irrevocably marred by sin, and if heaven is indeed a place of ineffable bliss and joy, why doesn't God take us to heaven immediately upon our conversion?' Or, perhaps, a sentiment from our darker moments: 'Why don't we take our own lives and simply hasten the inevitable ending?'

Have you ever thought this way? Of course, I am not speaking at this point about the person who is not a Christian. The non-Christian *lives* for this world. His investments, his passions, his interests and preoccupations, his affections – all his hopes and dreams are bound up with this world. Even when things turn for the worse, he still stakes his future on the hope that one day this life will get better. Correspondingly, his most frightening consideration is the day this life will end. But why is this prospect so fearful to him? Within his conscience exists the gnawing thought that after death there will be a moment of reckoning with his Creator. Hence, he holds on to this life with all the tenacity of a pit bull.

My concern at the moment, however, is for those of you who look to the future in confident expectation: people who, by virtue of your faith in the promises of the gospel, joyfully anticipate the final phase of your salvation. It is to you I pose the question: *Considering all there is to endure in this sin-cursed world* – the trials and disappointments, the heartbreaks and temptations, our withering bodies and fragmented relationships, the sin of other people and the ever-increasing awareness of our own sin – *what is it that keeps us from terminating our existence in this life so that we may be ushered into the next?*

A Sacred Mission

The Scriptures provide many answers to this question. The one that presses itself upon us from the passage we are considering, however, is that Jesus Christ has given us a mission to accomplish in this world. It is a mission given to every one of us; and, quite frankly, continued existence in this life as a Christian makes very little sense apart from it.

On the evening prior to his crucifixion, Jesus Christ tells His disciples He is going away and they cannot accompany Him. Why is this? His Father has assigned Him a specific mission: a mission that would, by predetermined design, involve leaving this world. But Jesus is equally emphatic about another thing: He has a specific mission for these men. The specific mission of Jesus Christ? To *leave this world* via the cross and all of its redemptive accomplishments so as to procure the gift of salvation for all who would come to believe in Him. The specific mission of the disciples? To *remain in this world* for the express purpose of declaring to it the saving benefits secured by the conquest of Jesus Christ. In other words, *His clarion call for them was to a worldly Christianity.*

This being the case, Jesus now turns His attention to praying for these men because He knows the sphere of their ministry is not an environment favorable to the things of God: 'I do not ask that you take them out of the world, but that you keep them from the evil one. They are not of the world, just as I am not of the world' (vv. 15-16). It is important to notice Jesus does not pray for disengagement from the world; His purpose for them is not a detached, monastic kind of Christianity. Quite the contrary, He requests of His Father: '... *while they remain in this world,* protect them from the power of the evil one.'

As this prayer unfolds we further discover that to accomplish their mission in this world *divine protection* is not the disciples' only need. They will also require the experience of *divine sanctification,* the very thing for which Jesus prays in verses 17-19. The structure of these three verses is simple to detect. In verse 17 we have *the request itself:* 'Sanctify them in the truth; your word is truth.' In verse 18, we have *the reason for the request:* 'As you sent me into the world, so I have sent them into the world.' And finally, in verse 19, we have *the basis for the request:* 'And for their sake I consecrate myself, that they also may be sanctified in truth.'

Why is this 'sanctification' a concern on the heart of our Lord? Why is it such a pressing issue? It is owing to the fact that Jesus is about to do to His disciples what His Father had done to Him: 'As you sent me into the world, so I have sent them into the world.' The verb translated 'sent' is the Greek word *apostello* – easily identified by its sound (*apostle*). It speaks of an official, authoritative sending. An apostle – a 'sent one' – is a person officially sent on a specific mission, bearing a particular authority by virtue of the one who sent him.

In the Gospel of John, Jesus frequently refers to Himself as the One 'sent' into the world. In this chapter alone, He speaks of the Father sending Him on five occasions. In keeping with this emphasis, the author of Hebrews labels Jesus as 'the *apostle* [emphasis added] ... of our confession' (Heb. 3:1). Jesus Christ, then, is the ultimate apostle, the 'sent one' *par excellence*, dispatched on a specific mission, bearing a unique authority by virtue of the One who sent Him. And now, in like manner, Jesus, 'the sent one,' would send His disciples: '*As* [emphasis added] you sent me into the world, so I have sent them into the world.' They, like Him, would be sent out officially to accomplish a specific mission, bearing a distinct authority by virtue of the One who sent them. Of course, in the full and final sense, this sending does not occur until John 20, subsequent to the resurrection. But so certain of the resurrection is Jesus that He speaks proleptically – as though it had *already taken place*. They would be apostles, sent into the world, authoritatively commissioned by Jesus Christ Himself.

And now, in this context, here is the principal point: *the extent to which they would be effective in the carrying out of their role (v. 18) would be directly proportional to the degree in which they had been sanctified by the truth (v. 17)*. This is the reason for the request of Jesus: He is sending them into the world to advance His cause, and unless they are sufficiently sanctified by means of the Christ-centered Scriptures ('the truth') their mission would be doomed from the start.

You may be aware of a new and popular word in our contemporary evangelical subculture. It is the term 'missional.' 'We need to become *missional*,' many exhort, often using this term as though they have invented an altogether novel concept. While it is most certainly true that our churches need to be missional – and that we, as individual Christians, must always seek to be missional – the fact is, one cannot be effectively missional without first being intentionally theological: 'Sanctify them in the truth, your word is truth,' the Lord prays. It assures us that gospel success does not depend on one's powers of creativity, the ability to plan and execute a program, or the use of marketing skills to make the Church satisfying to an unbeliever. Rather, effectiveness in gospel ministry rests on the extent to which Christ's 'sent ones' are set apart by the means of the Word of God. And yet, there is a reason for this request: 'As you sent me into the world, so I have sent them into the world.' The connection here is vital and must not be missed: this request of Jesus is a prayer of sanctification *for* gospel ministry, sanctification *for* engagement with the world. And so, while we cannot be missional without being theological, we must never be theological without being missional. In plain and simple terms: *we cannot hope to be authentically Christian without being meaningfully worldly.*

This Commission Is your Commission

'I see the connection you're making between these two verses,' you readily affirm. 'And I recognize this as the burden in Jesus' request. But, quite frankly, how is this relevant? What does any of this have to do with me?' By way of some extended application, this prayer encompasses you directly at two strategic points. The first is as follows: *this apostolic commission is your commission.*

'Oh,' you say, 'I know what you're pushing. It's the Great Commission given by Jesus at the conclusion of Matthew's Gospel':

Go therefore and make disciples of all nations, baptizing them in the name of the Father and of the Son and of the Holy Spirit, teaching them to observe all that I have commanded you. And behold, I am with you always, to the end of the age (Matt. 28:19-20).

21

'Yes, yes, yes, I am well-acquainted with this passage as I hear my pastor cite it nearly every week. I know it by heart.' But do you realize the Great Commission actually appears in all *four* Gospel accounts? In Mark's Gospel it reads as follows: 'Go into all the world and proclaim the gospel to the whole creation' (16:15). Luke writes that: '... the Christ should suffer and on the third day rise from the dead, and that repentance and forgiveness of sins should be proclaimed in his name to all nations ... You are witnesses of these things' (24:46-48). John's Gospel records it in its briefest form: 'As the Father has sent me, even so I am sending you' (20:21). Finally, it appears yet again in the book of Acts: '... you will be my witnesses in Jerusalem and in all Judea and Samaria, and to the end of the earth' (1:8).

At the risk of seeming pedantic, I draw these obvious references to your attention so I can now legitimately ask: Is it possible that a biblically informed Christian could ever misconstrue the primary mission of the Church of the living God? The Great Commission is repeated five times in the New Testament, and on each occasion it is the resurrected Christ doing the speaking! What's the point? If we are to give more than mere token consideration to the commands of Jesus Christ, we will find ourselves with no other alternative but to conclude that to be authentically Christian requires us to be meaningfully worldly – *that, in fact, Jesus Himself envisions no other kind of Christianity.*

You reply, 'But this commission by Jesus was originally given to the eleven disciples. One may grant that secondary application may be appropriate to people entering vocational ministry – a missionary, an evangelist, a pastor – but the original commission was made to the apostolic band.' Is this an accurate sentiment? Yes and no. To be sure, the record of the Great Commission in the Gospel of Matthew is addressed to the eleven disciples. In the Gospel of Luke, however, the call to go into the world is assigned to a much larger group of followers. This points to the fact that the apostolic commission belongs to all Christians. It is the principal reason we are here and not already in heaven. We exist for the sake of the gospel, and any misunderstanding at this point will inevitably lead the Christian to despair.

In this world we can never fully escape the effects of sin. To the contrary, as we are progressively conformed to the image of Christ, the awareness of sin's devastation, both to ourselves and other people, increasingly intensifies. Consequently, we are left to ponder why our good and kind heavenly Father keeps us in this world when the prospect of heaven is so much better. The answer is this: God has placed us here to be mouthpieces for Jesus Christ.

Until you understand this, my Christian friend, you will never know the true purpose for your existence in this world. Inevitably self-pity will become your indulgence of choice as you come to resent the disappointing life you believe God has given you. For this very reason we have tried to impress upon our children that life has not been given to them as an experiment in self-indulgence – the relentless pursuit of bigger houses, faster cars, shapely bodies, exotic vacations, and exhilarating sex. Rather, we exist as Christians in this world for the accomplishment of a mission. It is this very perspective we hear in the testimony of the apostle Paul:

> For to me to live is Christ, and to die is gain. If I am to live in the flesh, that means fruitful labor for me. Yet which I shall choose I cannot tell. I am hard pressed between the two. My desire is to depart and be with Christ, for that is far better. But to remain in the flesh is more necessary on your account. Convinced of this, I know that I will remain and continue with you all, for your progress and joy in the faith ... (Phil. 1:21-25).

In the light of the promise of heaven and unimpeded intimacy with Christ, Paul asserts that life in this world will prove senseless apart from the priority of personal investment in the gospel enterprise.

You have a mission as binding upon you as it was for the original eleven disciples: 'As you sent me into the world, so I have sent them into the world.' This is *your* commission. Do you feel the weightiness of it? This is not merely the commission of your pastor. This is the responsibility and privilege of every one who professes to be a follower of Jesus Christ.

The Sphere of your Mission Is the World

The second point of extended application is this: *the sphere of your mission is the world*. Acknowledging this, however, necessitates some wisdom from church history because, with relationship to this issue, evangelicals in nearly every generation (including ours) have succumbed to two practical distortions that have severely undercut our gospel effectiveness: cultural gluttony or cultural anorexia.

What is cultural gluttony? It is sinful compromise with the world: that is, *the consequence of being missional without being theological.* Often masked in the guise of desiring to win the world, Christians rabidly pursue likeness to the world. Over time, unfortunately, the world's values, objectives, and desires become *our* values, objectives, and desires. Cultural gluttony is the act of consuming the culture until it forms us.

As an American, let me tell you something of the cultural messages that bombard us every day – perhaps hundreds, even thousands, of times – via the radio, television, internet, or billboards as we drive along the motorway. For thirty years *Nike* has relentlessly advocated: 'Just do it.' (Don't think about it. Don't let anything or anyone stand in your way of doing it. Just do it.) *Burger King* avows: 'Sometimes you gotta break the rules.' *Bacardi Black Rum* (which advertises itself as 'The taste of the night') says: 'Some people embrace the night because the rules of the day do not apply.' *Easy Spirit* promises a shoe that 'conforms to your foot so you don't have to conform to anything.' *Ralph Lauren Safari* (a line of cologne and perfume) celebrates 'living without boundaries.' *Neiman Marcus* (a clothier chain) encourages its customers to relax because 'There are no rules here.' The *Outback Steakhouse*, a well-known eating establishment, boasts on the front cover of its menu: 'No rules.' These messages, and many others like them, bombard us incessantly – no rules, no boundaries, no standards of conformity – all, of course, as a consequence of our postmodern culture, which asserts: 'No truth.'

How has the Church of Jesus Christ withstood this cultural influence? Have we identified and eschewed it? Not hardly. For nearly thirty years American pastors have been assailed by church-growth experts seeking to convince them of the need to embrace a marketing strategy for ministry – that, in order to survive, they must now regard people as consumers to whom it must be said: 'Come and have it your way. How can we accommodate you? What are your felt needs? We'll never alienate, never offend, never bore, never convict – we'll never ask anything of you.' A leading advocate of this approach has said it matter-of-factly: 'It is critical that we keep in mind a fundamental principle of Christian communication: the audience, not the message, is sovereign.'[1] This is designer religion, allowing itself to be tailored to each personality. It gives, but never takes. It satisfies needs, but never asks for repentance. It offers mystery and asks for no service. It provides a sense of something *other*, without asking us to stand before that *Other*. It is the error of compromise – cultural gluttony – a pitfall into which the Church has frequently stepped, much to her own demise.

An alternative to which the Church has often succumbed in reaction is that of cultural anorexia: that is, *the consequence of being theological without being missional.*

1.   George Barna, *Marketing The Church*, p. 145.

It takes the form of a radical and decided withdrawal from the world. Since we are determined not to let the world shape us, we isolate, insulate, and withdraw. Before long the Church evolves into a kind of enclave, a ghetto, an island of irrelevant piety, and eventually we lose the ability to speak to non-Christians. Worse yet, our hearts become filled with a compassionless indifference toward such people.

Have you fallen prey to this? It occurs almost imperceptibly: often without intention. Do you have a meaningful relationship with any non-Christian person (other than a relative)? Can you recall the last time you shared a meal in your home with someone who was not a professing Christian? It is disturbing that some Christians actually believe the goal of parenting is to do everything possible to keep their children disengaged from the world. I profoundly disagree. The burden of Christian parents must be to prepare their children to engage the world with a mind filled with the Scriptures, a heart aflame with love for Jesus Christ, and a courage endowed by the Spirit of the living God.

The sphere of our mission is the world. This does not frighten me. To the contrary, it fills me with a sense of anticipation. It is a great day to be a Christian, a great moment to know the gospel. We are alive at a time when lives are being destroyed by sin as never before, and the truth belongs to us – the truth that can conquer any perplexity modernity or postmodernity may set before us. Consequently, I do not want my children growing up in a defensive posture. I want them to see themselves in the offensive position. *We have the gospel.* We have the promise God made to Abraham that in his seed all the families of the earth would be blessed. We have the fulfillment of that promise in Revelation 5, where we read that Jesus purchased human beings for God from every tribe and language and people and nation. We must, then, recapture the confidence of the hymn-writer:

> This is my Father's world;
> O let me ne'er forget
> that though the wrong seems oft so strong,
> God is the ruler yet.
> This is my Father's world;
> The battle is not done;
> Jesus who died shall be satisfied,
> and heaven and earth be one
> (Maltbie D. Babcock, 1901).

At this critical moment in history we must not lose our nerve and flee the culture, justifying ourselves in some expression of pseudo-piety. To the contrary, we must recognize that it is Jesus Himself who sends us into the culture: not in service to the culture – in the sense of helping it achieve its own ends – but in a divinely subversive way, infiltrating the culture with the kingdom of God and the gospel.

A Conviction Born of Experience

Why do I feel so passionately about this matter? It is the consequence of an epiphany I experienced about ten years ago in my own congregation. I took note of a group of young men and women, aged 16-18, who had grown up in professing Christian families. As I listened to them speak about unbelievers my heart was broken by the attitudes they displayed: the contempt, the disgust, the lack of compassion. It was clear they had no relationships with people outside the community of faith. Non-Christians were to be avoided at all costs.

How had this happened? Had I contributed to this? My wife (Lori) and I grieved that such a thing could occur within our own congregation, so contradictory was it to everything we believed ministry to be. We eventually became so burdened by this we removed our children from the private Christian school and enrolled them into the public school. We had no idea what opportunities for the gospel that strategic decision would stimulate for us.

Three months later, Lori was struck with a wonderful idea. Once a month, on a Friday evening, we would open our home to young people. The directions we gave to our children for these evenings were minimal: 1) invite as many friends as you like; 2) we will provide all the food and drink; and, 3) there is one ground rule: *no Christians*. Without a doubt these once-a-month Friday evenings became the most significant evangelistic endeavor in which we had ever engaged. It provided us with numerous opportunities to communicate the gospel to young people. Moreover, and quite unexpectedly, it created many opportunities to speak with parents who sought us out for friendship and, on occasion, counsel. A few of these displayed no interest in the gospel. Others evidenced some initial sensitivity to spiritual matters. Some confessed faith in Christ. Happily, many of these relationships continue to this present moment. Of course, only the great and final day will reveal the eternal consequences of this simple ministry. Nevertheless, its value for our family is that it created a context for us to carry out our mission in faithfulness to Jesus Christ. And – I might add – we have never been the same since.

'As you sent me into the world, so I have sent them into the world.' Jesus Christ was sent into the world. In like manner, Jesus Christ has now sent us into the world. Our 'sentness' is nothing less than an opportunity to imitate Him. It is a clarion call to a worldly Christianity. But this raises a critical question: How do we walk the razor's edge, avoiding both cultural gluttony and cultural anorexia? How do we engage the world meaningfully without ceasing to live Christianly?

2

Sanctify them in the truth; your word is truth
(John 17:17).

2

A Holy People

If our Christianity is not *worldly*, then it is not sufficiently Christian. But is this to imply that our worldliness cannot be altogether *Christian*? Jesus, on the one hand, tells us that God loves the world (John 3:16). James, on the other hand, exhorts us to keep 'unstained from the world,' insisting that 'friendship with the world is enmity with God' (James 1:27; 4:4). Are these statements antithetical? Is it possible to reconcile them? Can a person be simultaneously *Christian* and *worldly*?

What God Desires

God wants a holy people. About this there can be no question. He, who is altogether holy, desires image-bearers who reflect His own perfection of holiness. For example, God's word to ancient Israel concerned His passion for their holiness: 'I am the LORD your God. Consecrate yourselves therefore, and be holy, for I am holy' (Lev. 11:44). The apostle Peter, in turn, advances this to God's new covenant people: 'As obedient children, do not be conformed to the passions of your former ignorance, but as he who called you is holy, you also be holy in all your conduct' (1 Pet. 1:14-15). Christians serious about following Jesus Christ often find themselves in situations that compel them to ask: 'What is God's will for my life?' It is Paul the apostle who answers this in unambiguous terms: 'For this is the will of God, your sanctification' (1 Thess. 4:3). The writer of Hebrews speaks most boldly at this point: 'Strive for ... the holiness without which no one will see the Lord' (Heb. 12:14). Holiness, then, is not a matter of secondary importance: something for intermittent consideration. Rather, it is the *sine qua non* of authentic Christian spirituality – the one thing without which nothing else matters.

Let us be more definitive at this point. God does not desire a *moral* people; He desires a *holy* people. You ask: 'Is there really a difference between the two?' There is most certainly. It is the difference between the Pharisees – the most zealous of the parties of ancient Judaism during the late Second Temple period – and the Lord Jesus Christ. *They* were moral; *He* was holy. Morality is the negative concept, in that it defines itself in terms of what one refrains from doing. Its preoccupation is almost exclusively with externals. Holiness, by contrast, is the positive and holistic concept. While encompassing externals, its reach is far more penetrating and comprehensive. One may describe the difference as follows: the moral person abstains from wrong *actions* ... the holy person hates the very *thought* of wrongdoing. The moral person is preoccupied by what *people* perceive him to be ... the holy person is consumed with what *God* wants him to be. The moral person mindlessly adheres to a cold list of dos and don'ts ... the holy person ponders what brings greatest pleasure to his heavenly Father. The moral person keeps a meticulous record of his good deeds, expecting by them to win the favor of God ... the holy person grieves that nothing he ever does, even for God, is altogether free of sinful and selfish motive. Thus he recognizes every blessing from God as an expression of pure grace. The moral person lives by a self-determined definition of right and wrong and delights to impose it upon other people ... The holy person yields to the Word of God as the final authority, which, in turn, compels him to guard the silences of the Bible and, therefore, honor the freedoms these allow among those who serve the same Savior.

Sadly, our contemporary evangelical subculture is often morality-driven rather than holiness-driven. In my country it frequently expresses itself in the following kinds of sentiments: 'If only we could reinstitute prayer in public schools ... ' 'If only we could require the Ten Commandments to be posted on the walls of our legal institutions ...' 'If only we could elect more Christians to Congress and thus legislate against homosexual marriage ... ' But such emphases, albeit well-meaning, reveal a failure to comprehend the radical difference between moral reformation and God-authored regeneration. The moralist falls short precisely because he fails to appreciate that the gospel of transformation is far more powerful than the religion of prohibition. Contrarily, the biblical record steadily reveals that God fulfills his purposes in the world not through the means of a moral majority but a holy minority. Holiness, not morality, is God's desire for His people – and it is this for which our Lord Himself prays just hours prior to His own crucifixion.

Establishing the Context

What is the context of this prayer? The public ministry of the Son of God has concluded, as has His more intimate ministry with the Eleven. Together they leave the Upper Room and, by the Judean moonlight, make their way to a familiar spot: the Garden of Gethsemane. John indicates, however, that before crossing the Kidron Valley and entering the Garden, Jesus lifts His eyes to heaven and prays (cf. John 18:1; 17:1). What prompts this apparently spontaneous expression of prayer? John omits this detail. Of course, we do know these events are occurring during Passover week, a season in which thousands of lambs are being sacrificed in the Temple area. Moreover, the Jewish historian, Josephus, indicates the Kidron Brook served as the dumping site for the residual blood of the slaughtered lambs. It is quite possible the sudden sight of this blood – a graphic foreshadowing of His own violent death as the ultimate Passover Lamb – stopped Jesus in His tracks and aroused Him to prayer.

Its structure is easily identifiable: in verses 1-5 Jesus prays for Himself; in verses 6-19 Jesus makes petition for the eleven disciples (Judas having been dismissed); finally, in verses 20-26 his intercession broadens to include all who will come to embrace the apostolic gospel. The three verses presently occupying our attention emerge from the middle section: Jesus' prayer on behalf of the disciples. And from these verses we have considered *the reason* for His request: 'As you sent me into the world, so I have sent them into the world' (v. 18). To be authentically Christian requires us to be meaningfully worldly. But this, in turn, raises an exceedingly practical question: *How can we engage the world meaningfully without compromising the integrity of our Christianity?*

The answer to this question is found in the request itself: 'Sanctify them in the truth; your word is truth' (v. 17). According to Jesus, the disciples will need to be 'sanctified' for the sake of the mission to which He assigns them. In what manner is this relevant? Their mission has now been delegated to *us*. While we do not espouse a succession of apostolic authority, or a succession of apostolic office, we do affirm a succession of apostolic *mission*. As followers of Jesus Christ we bear a gospel ministry that is trans-generational. It stands to reason, then, if we are to fulfill our task in this world (v. 18), we too will need to be *sanctified* (v. 17). To more carefully understand what this means, let us ask four questions of this verse: 1) What does Jesus mean by the term 'sanctify'? 2) What instrument does God employ to accomplish this request? 3) Of whom does Jesus make this request? 4) For whom does Jesus make this request?

1. What does Jesus mean by the term 'sanctify'?

The word 'sanctify' belongs to a family of words that speak of holiness. Of course, the word 'holy' is often used as an adjective for God Himself. For example, He is 'the Holy One,' 'the most Holy One,' the God who is 'holy, holy, holy.' It is not merely to suggest that God is greater than everyone else, or distinguished by a stature of righteousness altogether unrivaled. Holiness is a way of saying that God is *transcendent:* that He is uniquely set apart and distinct from His creation. Accordingly, people (and even things!) uniquely set apart for God are said to be 'holy' or 'sanctified.'

Not long after Lori and I were married, we received an invitation to dinner. It was the Christmas season, and our friends had decorated their home in a way that was warm and festive. We especially took notice of their Christmas dishes – they were beautiful. We ourselves could not afford such dishes. I was still in seminary, earning only a few hundred dollars each month as a pastoral intern. Nevertheless, we decided to reallocate the money ordinarily spent on a Christmas tree toward a set of these Christmas dishes. In just a few years – along with the help of some generous family members – we had collected an entire set. They are not extraordinarily elegant, to be sure, but they have come to possess a great deal of meaning to us. Here is the point: we do not eat from these dishes every day, nor did we allow our children to play with them. In fact, we do not even use them on birthdays or anniversaries. To do so would profane them; it would make them common.

In fact, with the exception of a few special dinners during the Christmas season, these dishes are carefully boxed and placed on a high shelf in our garage so that no one can access them without a tall ladder and a long reach. They are, as it were, 'sanctified' dishes, uniquely set apart for and dedicated to a particular purpose.

In the Scriptures we find a similar phenomenon: people and things, uniquely set apart for God, being defined as 'holy' or 'sanctified.' For example, Aaron and his sons were 'sanctified' – set apart for the sacred duty of serving God as priests. The altar on which they offered sacrifices was 'sanctified' – uniquely dedicated to God for His purpose. This was also true of the priestly clothing – they were 'sanctified' garments. In fact, all the furnishings of the Tabernacle, and even the Tabernacle itself, were 'sanctified' – set apart from everything else for the distinct purpose assigned them by God. While it is accurate to assert that some texts associate ethical behaviors with holiness, we must always recognize them as the attendant consequences of having been uniquely devoted to God.

This reflects the burden of Jesus when He prays: '*Sanctify* [emphasis added] them.' That is: 'Set these men apart for a sacred purpose.' And what purpose is in view? Not one that is vaguely generic, but explicitly specific, articulated in verse 18: to engage the world for the sake of the gospel. In other words, the 'sanctification' for which Jesus prays is *a sanctification for mission*. To reinforce this meaning, one need only consider that earlier Jesus employs this same language with reference to Himself: that He is the one 'whom the Father consecrated ['sanctified'] and sent into the world' (v. 36).

What does Jesus mean by the term 'sanctify'? 'Set these men apart for the sacred purpose of sending them into the world.' Now if, as we have already seen, this commission of the eleven disciples (v. 18) has become our commission, it is incumbent upon us to recognize the *sacred nature* of this calling: that it is a consecration. Consequently, if we have no meaningful engagement with the world for the sake of the gospel, we are abdicating our identity as the 'set-apart' followers of Jesus Christ.

2.   *What instrument does God employ to accomplish this request?*

He uses *the truth*: 'Sanctify them in the truth.' To eliminate any possibility of ambiguity, Jesus defines the truth by which this sanctification occurs: 'your word is truth.' It is helpful to recall that, earlier this same evening, Jesus had distinctly referred to *Himself* as the truth: 'I am the way, and *the truth* [emphasis added], and the life' (John 14:6). Is this a coincidence – a connection between statements existing solely on the basis of a restricted vocabulary? Perhaps the reuse of this phrase is the consequence of a forgetful memory? Or is there an intended relationship between these statements? It was an extraordinary claim, and highly implausible that the disciples would have lost its impression so quickly. Its echoes return as Jesus again uses this language – 'the truth' – to now refer to the Father's Word.

Most likely, these statements should be understood as

mutually interpreting. When we read John 17:17, then, we are to understand that while Jesus is setting forth the Scriptures as the efficient instrument of sanctification, their intention is not adequately comprehended until we appreciate their Christo-centric emphasis: *they are the truth about this one who is the truth.* Therefore, the experience that effectively sanctifies the people of God for their sacred work of being sent into the world is immersion into the Word of God – a Word that is distinctly Christ-centered.

Moreover, it is worth noting that as Jesus amplifies this statement He does not employ a mere adjective: 'Your word is *true.*' Rather, He uses the substantive: 'your word is *truth* [emphasis added].' 'But is there really a difference,' you ask. 'Is it not an accurate statement to assert that the Bible is true?' Of course, it *is* an accurate statement to assert that the Bible is true. The problem is that such an assertion does not communicate *comprehensively and ultimately*. Were Jesus to merely claim – 'your word is true' – doing so would leave him susceptible to criticism: 'On what basis can you assert the Bible to be true? What is the criteria by which you test the truthfulness of the Scriptures?' Such a claim leaves open the possibility of a higher standard of truth to which the Bible merely conforms. By contrast, when Jesus avows, 'your word is *truth* [emphasis added],' He certainly infers the accuracy and reliability of the Scriptures, *but He does so by unambiguously affirming them as the ultimate definition of truth*. The Scriptures are the criteria, the standard, and reference point by which everything else is to be measured. And here, in this context, they are defined particularly as the instrument of sanctification: a concept, it must be added, not confined to this passage alone:

> The law of the LORD is perfect, *reviving the soul*; the testimony of the LORD is sure, *making wise the simple*; the precepts of the LORD are right, *rejoicing the heart*; the commandment of the LORD is pure, *enlightening the eyes* (Ps. 19:7-8, emphasis added).

> For the word of God is living and active, sharper than any two-edged sword, piercing to the division of soul and of spirit, of joints and of marrow, and discerning the thoughts and intentions of the heart (Heb. 4:12).

> All Scripture is breathed out by God and profitable for teaching, for reproof, for correction, and for training in righteousness, that the man of God may be competent, equipped for every good work (2 Tim. 3:16-17).

If sanctification is our aim, God's instrument of choice is the Christ-centered Scriptures.

Can you imagine the consequences that would have befallen Jesus' disciples had they sought to make known the message of Christianity apart from the sanctifying grace for which He here prays? From their earliest moments of missionary endeavor, they would engage in violent confrontation with the enemy himself – the father of lies – who would perpetuate his all-too-familiar work of corrupting the Word of God, thus distorting the exclusive message of salvation. How could they ever defend the gospel if they themselves are not saturated in its truths, including the various life consequences that result from it? How could they defend the Church against the heresies seeking to destroy her – the denial of the resurrection of Jesus Christ from the dead, for example, that Paul must confront in 1 Corinthians 15? How could they impact the Mediterranean world with the gospel if they are ill-prepared to counteract the denial of justification by faith alone prevalent among the Galatians? What success could they expect to experience if they prove inadequate in their capacities to correct the denials of the full deity or the full humanity of Jesus Christ? How could they rectify the Corinthian confusion regarding the Holy Spirit if they themselves are not 'sanctified' by means of the truth?

And what of the various ethical challenges that will emerge in the early Christian congregations? What action will they take with the man who has become sexually intimate with his father's wife (1 Cor. 5)? Or with the Christians in Thessalonica who refuse work, ostensibly because they are anticipating the Lord's return (2 Thess. 3)? What about Christians who engage in lawsuits against other Christians? What about Christian husbands who exploit their wives – and Christian wives who refuse their husbands' leadership? What about parents who refuse to assume proper responsibility for their children – and children who defy their parents? What about Christian employees who refuse obedience to their non-Christian employers – and Christian employers who exploit their employees? What is to be done with 'mature' believers who expect to openly exercise their freedoms without regard for the difficulties and temptations this may pose for their brothers and sisters? The disciples of Jesus are being sent into the world to preach the gospel – the message of his death, burial, and resurrection. By the grace of God, many to whom they preach will be saved. What, then, are they to do with the multiplicity of problems these newly saved sinners bring into the church? It is precisely for this reason Jesus prays for them: 'Sanctify them by the truth, your word is truth.' It will be the strength of their grip on the truth – *or the strength of the truth's grip on them* – that will determine the measure of their success. Fifteen centuries later it proved to be true once again, as Luther himself said of the Reformation's influence:

> And yet while I was asleep, or drinking Wittenberg beer with my Philip Melanchthon and Amsdorf, the Word inflicted greater injury on popery than prince or emperor ever did. I did nothing, the Word did everything.

Are our present contexts of ministry altogether different from those in the first century – or the sixteenth? Are we not repeatedly confronted with very similar situations? Though packaged in a more modern (or postmodern!) kind of wrapping, similar challenges eventually cycle around to confront us. Once again we have professing evangelicals denying the doctrine of substitutionary atonement, advocating universal reconciliation, rejecting Jesus Christ as the exclusive way to God, diminishing the objective authority of the sacred text, disregarding the significance of the Church.

As a Christian, you may on occasion be tempted to ask: 'Why is it always the *Bible* with our pastors? Why do they insist that preaching is not preaching unless it is the exposition of the Word? Why must all our classes and studies and discipleship ministries be steeped in Scripture? Why should we labor to ensure that our congregational music is a vehicle through which to communicate the truth?' The answer to each of these questions is the same: It is because 'the truth' is the divinely appointed instrument by which a Christian is sanctified. It is because effectiveness in our mission is altogether dependent upon the degree to which we are sanctified by the truth. It was stated earlier: *we must never be theological without being missional* – 'As you sent me into the world, so I have sent them into the world.' What is equally true is this: *we cannot be missional without being theological* – 'Sanctify them in the truth; your word is truth.'

3. Of whom does Jesus make this request?

As verse-by-verse we trace back the various antecedent pronouns ('your,' 'you,' etc), we finally discover the definitive answer to this question in verse 11: 'Holy Father.' This, then, is the One to whom Jesus directs His request in verse 17. Why state the painfully obvious? To make clear that, while sanctification is brought about by the instrumentality of the Word of God, the actual effectiveness of the Word requires a work only God can perform. Without hesitation, we readily affirm the Word of God as the *instrument* of sanctification. We must equally acknowledge, however, that God Himself is the *agent* of sanctification. The sacred Word possesses a resident life, but by itself it does not beget life. For a person to be sanctified by the Word, God Himself must make its inherent power effectual.

The Bible is not God. We do not worship the Bible. We worship the God who animates the Bible so that its truth changes us. The Word is the scalpel – God is the surgeon. The Word is the tool – God is the craftsman. The Word is the instrument – God is the virtuoso. It is true that sanctification will never happen apart from the Word, but the Word itself will never sanctify until God Himself animates it. This is made obvious by Jesus' request, which clearly implies dependence upon a divine work. Equally obvious is the fact that the apostolic Christians emulated this dependence on God by devoting themselves 'to *prayer* [emphasis added] and to the ministry of the word' (Acts 6:4).

This, too, must be our pattern. Are we seeking to study the Scriptures for ourselves? Are we preparing to sit under the ministry of the preached Word? Are we discussing the Bible during scheduled occasions of family worship? In each and every setting our dependence upon the direct and immediate work of God for sanctification is absolute. To be sure, when sanctification occurs it will owe itself to the fact that the Word of God has been used. But on such occasions the one who has wielded it is the God of the Word. Jesus makes this request of God Himself, the One who alone can use this Word to sanctify.

4. For whom does Jesus make this request?
The text says: 'Sanctify *them* [emphasis added].' This

petition of Jesus is undeniably and intentionally focused. It is not a petition made on behalf of all people everywhere. It reflects an appropriate narrowness that was explicitly introduced by Jesus in verse 9. Referring to His original disciples, He says: 'I am praying for them. I am not praying for the world but for those whom you have given me, for they are yours.' *Initially*, Jesus makes this request on behalf of those who had been given to Him by divine prerogative. 'So does this request have any bearing on us?' you ask. Take note of verse 20: 'I do not ask for these only, but also for those who will believe in me through their word.'

This prayer for sanctification includes you if you are a Christian. Of course, this implies that the sending includes you as well. It is how you fulfill God's purpose for your life. It is how you maintain a vibrant Christianity while being meaningfully worldly. Once again, God desires holiness, not mere morality: in this case, being set apart for the sacred purpose of invading the world with the gospel. Jesus Himself prays for this holiness – a holiness accomplished by the direct power of God Himself displayed through the instrumentality of His Word.

The Decisive Question

Are you immersing yourself in the Christ-centered Scriptures? Are you doing so steadily and consistently? I am not asking if you own a Bible. In the West we are inundated with Bibles – innumerable versions and editions of all shapes, sizes, textures, and colors – each designed to satisfy an individual's esthetic sense. Nor am I asking if you acknowledge the Bible's authority, sufficiency, and infallibility. My question is more experiential: Are you immersing yourself in the Christ-centered Scriptures? Have you positioned your life so you are steadily under the influence of the Word of God? Are you in a church committed to the preaching of the Word, offering various studies designed to illuminate the Word, conducting worship services distinguished by the singing of the Word? Are you personally feeding on the Scriptures, devouring and consuming them? Is this work of sanctification occurring within you?

This book contains
the mind of God, the state of man,
the way of salvation, the doom of sinners,
and the happiness of believers.
Its doctrine is holy, its precepts are binding,
its histories are true, and its decisions immutable.
Read it to be wise, believe it to be safe, and practise it to be holy.
It contains light to direct you,
food to support you, and comfort to cheer you.
It is the traveller's map, the pilgrim's staff,
the pilot's compass, the soldier's sword,
and the Christian's charter.
Here heaven is opened and the gates of hell disclosed.
Christ is its grand subject,
our good its design,
and the glory of God its end.
It should fill the memory,

rule the heart, and guide the feet.
Read it slowly, frequently, and prayerfully.
It is a mine of wealth,
health to the soul, and a river of pleasure.
It is given to you here in this life,
will be opened at the judgment,
and is established forever.
It involves the highest responsibility,
will reward the greatest honor,
and condemn all who trifle with its contents.

If our Christianity is not *worldly*, then it is not sufficiently Christian. But is this to imply that our worldliness cannot be altogether *Christian*? Not at all. So how can we engage the world meaningfully without compromising the integrity of our Christianity? Listen to the prayer of Jesus: 'Sanctify them in the truth; your word is truth.'

3

*And for their sake I consecrate myself, that they
also may be sanctified in truth*
(John 17:19).

3

An Effective Redemption

The preaching of the cross,
the preaching of the death of the Lord Jesus Christ on that cross,
is the very heart and center of the Christian gospel and the
Christian message.
Put that in the center, place it in the front,
proclaim it above everything else.
D. MARTYN LLOYD-JONES

Leave out the cross and you have killed the religion of Jesus.
Atonement by the blood of Jesus is not an arm of Christian truth,
it is the heart of it.
CHARLES HADDON SPURGEON

Christ is to us just what his cross is.
All that Christ was in heaven or on earth was put into what he did there.
On this the whole Church rests.
If you move faith from that center
you have driven the nail into the Church's coffin;
the Church is then doomed to death and it is only a matter of time
until she expires.
P.T. FORSYTH

> A Christianity which is not cross-centered
> is not Christianity at all.
>
> LEON MORRIS

> For the word of the cross is folly to those who are perishing,
> but to us who are being saved it is the power of God ...
> For I decided to know nothing among you
> except Jesus Christ and him crucified.
>
> PAUL THE APOSTLE

Christianity is a religion of the cross. Not a mystical fetish with a delicate ornament to adorn our appearance, rather, the cross is the symbol of everything Jesus Christ accomplished for us in His redeeming work. Christians, therefore, are a people of the cross. Of all the messages we proclaim, the cross occupies the pre-eminent place, and any other message we declare makes sense only to the extent it intersects with this most important message. We sing of the cross. We survey the wondrous cross. We extol the power of the cross. We stand beneath the cross. We plead with Jesus to keep us near the cross. It is where the purchase price was paid for our spiritual freedom. Here reconciliation was achieved between two apparently irreconcilable parties – God and humanity – because poised between the two with His outstretched arms was a mediator spanning the chasm of separation. We are not ashamed of the cross. We love the cross. We boast in the cross. We are held captive by the cross. Why? Because every blessing we receive from God was secured on the cross. It is this fact to which Jesus now appeals in His request to His Father on behalf of His followers.

As we have seen, *the request itself* is simple and straightforward: 'Sanctify them' (that is, 'set apart these men for a sacred purpose'). To accomplish this, the Father will appropriate an indispensable instrument: 'the truth.' *The reason for this request* is equally clear: 'As you sent me into the world, so I have sent them into the world.' In imitation of Jesus Himself, these men have been assigned a mission to accomplish: to enter into and engage the world with the gospel. Apart from the aforementioned sanctification, however, their effectiveness would be immediately neutralized, given the hostility of the world, the wily nature of the enemy, and the unholy undertow of their own residual sin. To be successful in advancing the gospel would necessitate a work only God Himself could perform: the experience of sanctification effected through the instrumentality of the Scriptures.

One final question remains: *What is the basis for this request?* On what grounds could Jesus beseech His Father to 'sanctify' these men? Was it owing to their inherent goodness and stellar faithfulness? Perhaps they deserved this blessing by virtue of their impeccable commitment and praiseworthy obedience? Not at all! The disciples were exceedingly fallen men, in no way deserving of such gracious intervention. Ironically, some of their most notorious failures lie only moments ahead. The only basis, therefore, upon which Jesus could petition His Father for sanctifying grace on their behalf was that He would *earn* it for them on the cross: that the work of *redemption* would provide the basis upon which this request for *sanctification* is made.

Jesus says in verse 19: 'And for their sake I consecrate [sanctify] myself.' For what purpose does He set Himself apart? The sacred purpose for which God sent Him into the world – a recurring theme throughout the fourth Gospel – *Jesus sets Himself apart for the cross*. But why does He do this? So that His request, articulated in verse 17, may now be granted: 'that they also may be sanctified in truth' (v. 19). It is here we discover that this gracious work of 'sanctification for mission' will be secured on the basis of Jesus' own act of self-sanctification: that His redeeming death on the cross would purchase the grace He here implores His Father to dispense. It is truly an amazing expression of His love, filling us with a sense of certain expectation. Nevertheless, it is only upon closer scrutiny of this verse that we can begin to approximate the significance of what Jesus is saying. We see here three very important qualities in this 'consecration' of Jesus Christ.

A Voluntary Consecration

First and foremost, it is plainly evident that this 'consecration' of Jesus Christ is *voluntary*. How do we arrive at this conclusion? Jesus does not employ the *passive voice* in verse 19 – (*e.g.* 'I am consecrated,' or 'I have been consecrated,' or 'I will be consecrated') – as if to highlight Himself as the one *receiving* the action in view. Rather, He uses the *active voice* so as to insist that this 'consecration' is something *He Himself will do* – 'I consecrate myself.' Accordingly, there must never be the slightest hint of passivity when consideration is given to Jesus' cross work, for the simple reason He was never more proactive than when He surrendered Himself to crucifixion. He was not drafted for the task. He willingly enlisted for the express purpose of accomplishing it: 'Behold, I have come to do your will, O God, as it is written of me in the scroll of the book' (Heb. 10:7). Jesus was not a victim. He was a volunteer. He was not coerced or manipulated. He was not dispatched to earth against His will. No one dictated to Him. No power moved Him. No prayer invited Him. No welcome awaited Him. He came *voluntarily* – a theme about which a wide range of Scriptures are explicit:

> For this reason the Father loves me, because I lay down my life ... No one takes it from me, but I lay it down *of my own accord* [emphasis added] (John 10:17, 18).

> And the life I now live in the flesh I live by faith in the Son of God, who loved me and *gave himself* [emphasis added] for me (Gal. 2:20).

> And walk in love, as Christ loved us and *gave himself* [emphasis added] up for us (Eph. 5:2).

> Have this mind among yourselves, which is yours in Christ Jesus, who, though he was in the form of God, did not count equality with God a thing to be grasped, but *made himself* nothing, taking the form of a servant, being born in the likeness of men. And being found in human form, he *humbled himself* by becoming obedient to the point of death, even death on a cross (Phil. 2:5-8, emphasis added).

> He has no need, like those high priests, to offer sacrifices
> daily, first for his own sins and then for those of the
> people, since he did this once for all when he *offered up
> himself* [emphasis added] (Heb. 7:27).

Of his own volition, God incarnate *consecrated Himself.*
He yielded Himself to the most degrading of indignities.
He submitted Himself to the vilest of reproaches. He
surrendered Himself to unspeakable tortures. And worse
by far, He consecrated Himself as the bull's-eye for his
Father's wrath against sin, epitomized by the cry of
dereliction from the cross: 'My God, my God, why have
you forsaken me?' (Matt. 27:46).

Can you conceive of such sacrifice? Can you fathom
one who would embrace such sacrifice willingly and
voluntarily? It is the *voluntary nature of His sacrifice* that
powerfully reveals the greatness of His love. Love always
bears a richer, deeper quality when it is self-initiated and
free, springing spontaneously from its subject rather than
being coerced by its object. The art of romance teaches us
this. When a husband says 'I love you' to his wife's complaint
regarding his persistent neglect of verbal affection, his
dutiful response (like that of an obedient poodle!) leaves
her altogether unsatisfied. But when such an expression
of love is unexpectedly and spontaneously conveyed, it
effects an impression of far greater significance.

Had the Son of God been forced into this world
– driven to His death on the cross – our amazement
at His love would not have been nearly as grand. But
when we become acquainted with His willingness, that

He voluntarily surrendered Himself as a substitutionary sacrifice, we are overwhelmed: amazed at the intensity and infinite capacity of such love. Is this not the distinguishing feature of the Wesley hymn so dear to us?

> *He left his Father's throne above—*
> *so free, so infinite his grace—*
> *humbled himself, so great his love,*
> *and bled for all his chosen race.*
> *'Tis mercy all, immense and free,*
> *for O my God it found out me.*
> *Amazing love! How can it be*
> *that thou my God shouldst die for me?*
> (Charles Wesley 1738).

Such love, in turn, evokes a reverberation. It awakens our love, precipitating instinctive replies of faith and obedience and worship – a Christian life as a response to grace.

A Specific Consecration

Secondly, this 'consecration' of Jesus is *specific*. For whom does Jesus set apart Himself as a sacrificial offering? The text says: 'for *their* [emphasis added] sake I consecrate myself.' But to whom does 'their' refer? The answer is evident when we discover the group against whom 'their' ('they,' 'them,') is repeatedly set in contrast:

> I have manifested your name to the people whom you gave me out of the *world* [emphasis added]. Yours they were, and you gave them to me (v. 6).

59

I am not praying for the *world* [emphasis added] but for those whom you have given me, for they are yours (v. 9).

I have given them your word, and the *world* has hated them because they are not of the *world* (v. 14, emphasis added).

I do not ask that you take them out of the *world* [emphasis added], but that you keep them from the evil one (v. 15).

They are not of the *world* [emphasis added] (v. 16).

I have sent them into the *world* [emphasis added] (v. 18).

Throughout the prayer's entirety 'their,' 'them,' 'they' – the disciples of Jesus – are set in opposition to 'the world.'

John 17 has been frequently described: 'The High Priestly Prayer Of Jesus Christ.' This is not ill-founded, as the unfolding of the chapter makes clear. Two primary functions defined the Old Testament high priest: 1) making prayerful intercession; and, 2) making sacrificial atonement. Corresponding to these two priestly tasks was a specific group of people for whom they were made: *the people of Israel*. When the high priest gave his attention to intercession, his efforts were focused on the covenant community. In like manner, when he entered the Holy of Holies to offer an atoning sacrifice, he did not do so for the Amorites, Perizzites, Hivites, and Hittites. Rather, those for whom he interceded and made atonement were one and the same, represented by his breastplate into which was embedded twelve stones representing God's people. The two priestly functions were co-extensive.

Jesus Christ is the typological fulfillment of the Old Testament priestly office, the ultimate high priest who consummates the dual priestly function dimly foreshadowed by the old covenant priests. So we ask: For whom does this greater high priest make prayerful intercession? 'I am praying for *them*. I am not praying for the *world* but for *those whom you have given me*' (v. 9, emphasis added). Jesus' intercession is specific: He prays for those given to Him by divine prerogative. Accordingly, for whom does Jesus exercise the second priestly function—making sacrificial atonement? The text is unambiguous: 'for *their* [emphasis added] sake I consecrate myself.' His priestly work proves to be co-extensive. Hence, it is evident the atoning sacrifice of Jesus is specific.

One can hear this same specificity in several New Testament passages. For example, consider the angel's familiar words to Joseph: 'She will bear a son, and you shall call his name Jesus, for he will save *his people* [emphasis added] from their sins' (Matt. 1:21). Listen afresh to the strong exhortation Paul makes to Christian husbands:

> Husbands, love *your* wives, as Christ loved *the church* and gave himself up for *her*, that he might sanctify *her*, having cleansed *her* by the washing of water with the word, so that he might present *the church* to himself in splendor, without spot or wrinkle or any such thing, that she might be holy and without blemish. In the same way husbands should love *their* wives (Eph. 5:25-28, emphasis added).

A husband is to love his wife in a manner specific and exclusive to her. Why? The Apostle justifies this lofty demand by grounding it in the love Jesus has specifically for the Church. But how, in particular, has this specificity distinguished itself? Jesus surrendered His life *for her*. His is a specific love, evidenced by a specific death.

This same specificity is heard in the worship occurring in heaven. In the apocalyptic vision recorded in Revelation 5, John sees a scroll in the hand of God. He begins to weep, however, because a universal unworthiness prevents its opening, thereby inhibiting the inauguration of its contents. But John is told to cease from despair because one *is* qualified to unseal the scroll – a lion who, paradoxically, is seen as a lamb. At the recognition of his worthiness, evidenced by the mere taking up of the scroll, celestial worship immediately erupts:

> And when he had taken the scroll, the four living creatures and the twenty-four elders fell down before the Lamb, each holding a harp, and golden bowls full of incense, which are the prayers of the saints. And they sang a new song, saying, 'Worthy are you to take the scroll and to open its seals, for you were slain, and by your blood you ransomed people for God *from* [emphasis added] every tribe and language and people and nation ...' (Rev. 5:8-9).

Many beneficial insights could be gleaned from a consideration of this heavenly poetry. In particular, however, is the significance of the preposition 'from' (in

Greek it is the partitive *ek*, meaning 'out of'). The angelic worshipers do not sing of the Lamb: 'By your blood you redeemed people for God – that is, every tribe and language and people and nation.' More precisely, they sing: 'By your blood you redeemed people for God *out of* every tribe and language and people and nation.' The specificity in these lyrics of redemption is plainly evident.

Some may reply by asserting the Lamb's accomplishments are potentially sufficient to save a billion worlds of sinners. That the atonement includes a universal provision seems to be a faithful acknowledgement of certain biblical texts. With equal vigor, however, the faithful Bible student must acknowledge other texts that clearly establish a specific focus far more definite than the provision of a mere potential atonement for all. It is this distinct specificity Jesus has in view in John 17: 'And *for their sake* [emphasis added] I consecrate myself.'

A Purposeful Consecration

Finally, this 'consecration' of Jesus is *purposeful*, distinguished by an intended efficacy. From the cross His pronouncement of victory was explicit: 'It is finished.' Does this declaration suggest mere possibility or potentiality? It avows the successful accomplishment of a mission.

In His death on the cross, Jesus purchased a full and complete salvation for His people. Among other benefits, it includes justification – a right-standing before God on the basis of Jesus' righteousness credited to the believer. It encompasses glorification – a consummated eternal life in the new creation, including a resurrected body. In this context, however, the principal purpose of Jesus' self-consecration concerns sanctification – being set apart by the means of truth for a distinct purpose assigned by God. Jesus prays: 'And for their sake I consecrate myself, that they also may be sanctified in truth.' How glorious to recognize that Jesus will purchase the very grace He beseeches His Father to dispense! And, of course, we must not fail to remember the ultimate objective for this sanctification: 'As you sent me into the world, so I have sent them into the world' (v. 18). For this reason, a Christian disengaged from the world is a colossal contradiction – *especially when this occurs in the name of piety*. It is no mere disregard of the task assigned to us by Jesus. It is far worse. Disengagement seeks to invalidate the sanctifying benefits Jesus won for us at the cross.

A Tale Of Two Cities by Charles Dickens is a story of two men, set during the stormy days of the French Revolution. The first, Charles Darnay, is a man of great dignity and unimpeachable character: a model of humanity at its very best. The second, Sydney Carton, is his stark antithesis: a debauched human being devoid of any redeeming virtue. Though irreconcilably dissimilar, their lives are unexpectedly linked together by two features: firstly, they bear to one another an uncanny physical resemblance; and, secondly, they are each in love with the same woman – the woman who eventually marries Charles Darnay.

As the early days of the Revolution unwind, French aristocrats are sought out, arrested, and summarily slaughtered. Darnay himself is imprisoned, for no other reason than his aristocratic bloodline. Week after week, month after month pass as he languishes in anticipation of his turn at 'the national razor' – the guillotine. Every day his beloved wife travels to the same location on a street corner where, if she elevates her vision to the precise spot, she can glimpse into the window of her husband's jail cell, hoping beyond hope to see him. From an unseen alley, the dissolute Sydney Carton is also there – each day – voyeuristically observing this woman he loves.

As the day of Darnay's execution becomes imminent, Carton unexpectedly conceives a plan. He gains admittance to Darnay's jail cell and, without his knowledge, serves Darnay a drink that drugs him into unconsciousness. To play the imposter, Carton quickly exchanges his clothes for Darnay's, and then appropriately adjusts his hair. Having calmed himself, he beckons the jailer who removes the insensible Darnay, now dressed as Sydney Carton. The apparent Carton – Darnay in reality – is placed in a horse-drawn carriage with his wife and daughter, given travel papers imprinted with Sydney Carton's name, and is whisked out of Paris, and finally out of France, before ever awakening to consciousness. In his place, Sydney Carton is taken to the site of execution where he is sacrificed as Charles Darnay, an enemy of the Revolution. But why does Carton exchange his life for Darnay's? Because of his great love for a woman. Dickens ends the story with his sacrificial lamb reciting these words: 'It is a far, far better thing that I do than I have ever done. It is a far, far better rest that I go to than I have ever known.'

It is a 'consecration' that is voluntary, specific, and purposeful. In one significant way, however, this picture of ultimate sacrifice profoundly deviates from the Christian gospel: Dickens's sacrifice suits our sense of tolerability in that it *deserves* to be made. The sinner *appropriately dies* for the saint. The unjust *appropriately dies* for the just. The worthless *appropriately dies* for the worthy. The scandalous nature of the cross, however, is that the very opposite occurs. The saint *astonishingly dies* for the sinner. The just *astonishingly dies* for the unjust. The worthy *astonishingly dies* for the worthless – the one making the sacrifice is of infinitely greater value than those for whom His sacrifice is made. We must never forget the stature of the One who fashioned these words in his mouth – 'for their sake I consecrate myself.' And so, rightly we sing:

> Guilty, vile and helpless we,
> Spotless Lamb of God was he,
> Full atonement!—can it be?
> *Hallelujah, what a Savior!*
> (Philip Paul Bliss 1875).

Are you truly acquainted with the cross work of Jesus Christ? Is it the single most important thing in your life? Have you paused recently to ponder the magnitude of its accomplishments – and the majesty of the One who was once fixed upon it? Have you experienced its saving and sanctifying benefits? There is no other avenue to eternal life. There is no other means to the forgiveness of sins. On the basis of the accomplishments of Jesus Christ, turn away from your sin and the idolatry of yourself. Embrace this Savior. I can assure you that, because of the cross, He will receive you. And I can assure you that, because of the cross, God will sanctify you for His own sacred purpose.

Jesus Christ has died to make you a worldly Christian.

4

Since then we have a great high priest who has passed through the heavens, Jesus, the Son of God, let us hold fast our confession. For we do not have a high priest who is unable to sympathize with our weaknesses, but one who in every respect has been tempted as we are, yet without sin. Let us then with confidence draw near to the throne of grace, that we may receive mercy and find grace to help in time of need (Heb. 4:14-16).

4

Our Sympathetic Resonance

I love baseball. Though not nearly as barbaric as rugby – the sport of choice in Wales – it is *America's* pastime. There is nothing quite like the exhilaration I feel when, having given my ticket to the usher and stepping through the turnstile, I walk out from underneath the dark overhang and catch the first glimpse of the field itself. It never ceases to take my breath away – the expansive green grass spanning the outfield, the smooth red clay blanketing the infield, the sparkling white lines demarcating the diamond! If the *sights* were not enough, there are the *sounds* of baseball – the echoing pop of a fastball in the catcher's glove, the distinctive crack of swinging wood against a pitched ball, the thunderous explosion of the crowd when an umpire bellows 'Strike three.' And, of course, there are the *tastes* of baseball – the prerequisite peanuts and their empty shells at my feet, the hot coffee at night games that scald my tongue, the sugary taste of my son's pink lips from the cotton candy.

In the not-too-distant past, I had the opportunity to see the Seattle Mariners play baseball at Safeco Field. As I enjoyed yet another game, absorbing every bit of the sights and sounds and tastes, I said to myself: 'Art, you *are* a worldly Christian!' But what did I mean? *I am exceedingly thankful for the privilege of being a live human being in this world.* Baseball at Safeco Field is just one of many reasons for this gratitude. I recently listened to the intermezzo from *Cavalleria Rusticana* and was again reminded of the overpowering effect of musical beauty. Not too long ago I read a novel by P. D. James and was spellbound by her masterful use of the English language. Some months ago I came across a volume of Ansel Adams's photographs that absorbed me for nearly an hour. Have you seen Kenneth Branagh perform *Hamlet*? Have you read Harper Lee's *To Kill A Mockingbird*? Have you listened to Arturo Sandoval improvise on the trumpet?

Sports, music, literature, art, drama – I am not ashamed to confess myself a worldly Christian. I love the created realm. I have no appetite for a Christianity that, in the name of spirituality, seeks disengagement from this world. The Scriptures declare this world to be the creation of God, existing for God, and that its final redemption is made certain by the fact that, in Jesus Christ, God Himself has entered this world as a flesh-and-blood human being: moreover, that Jesus Christ has conquered creation's enemies by means of a *bodily* resurrection. Accordingly, the hope for the Christian is not a wraithlike future, but an existence that is red-blooded and earthy: one defined by resurrection. To be sure, every genuine Christian eagerly anticipates full and complete detachment from sin. But the aim of salvation is *not* the elimination of our humanity – that we might be made ethereally angelic. It is the eradication of our fallenness – that we might be made holistically human. We will not exist ultimately as saved *souls*, redeemed *ghosts*. Rather, owing to the accomplishments of Jesus Christ, we will be saved *human beings* living eternally in a re-created world, possessing a sinless physicality indicative of an existence that is truly and fully human.

It must not surprise us, then, that Jesus' intention for His followers is a meaningful engagement with this world – that theirs would be a *worldly* Christianity. But a 'worldliness' that is decidedly and distinctly Christian will not, in most cases, be received enthusiastically. Presently, our world is marred by fallen influences in direct contradiction to the gospel. How does the world respond to this contradiction? It often seeks to silence it – sometimes most egregiously. Consequently, professing Christians may begin to ponder their allegiance to Jesus Christ: Is confessing Him commensurate with the cost?

This was the dilemma plaguing the Hebrew Christians. Under extraordinary social pressure (generated by the dominant Roman culture and their own ethnic subculture), they were living with the temptation to relinquish their commitment to Jesus Christ. One can easily imagine their various musings:

Maybe we should loosen our grip on the gospel – just a bit. After all, it does divide people.

A confession of Christianity separates family members – and that can't be a good thing.

Shouldn't we tone down the rhetoric – learn a little political correctness? Perhaps we've been a bit over the top – a little too exclusive in our commitment to Jesus.

In the face of these kinds of rationalizations – and the spiritual catastrophes they may birth – the Hebrew writer firmly articulates his word of exhortation: 'let us hold fast our confession' (Heb. 4:14b). He may be hearkening back to the occasion of his listeners' baptism, when they publicly confessed Jesus as Lord: 'Despite all pressure to the contrary, you must not renounce your acknowledgement of Jesus Christ. You must hold on to Him without wavering, come what may.' To motivate them toward this persevering faithfulness, he calls specific attention to Jesus as their 'great high priest.' In the language of the Old Testament, the title 'high priest' means literally: 'great priest.' To now entitle Jesus 'a great high priest' would effectively convey to these Hebrew Christians a priest who bears a distinct and unsurpassed superiority: that Jesus is a 'great, great priest' – that is, the greatest of all priests. But what is it that distinguishes His superiority to all others? Keeping in mind the context, what defines Jesus to be so pre-eminently great that a Christian should endure any sacrifice to maintain allegiance to Him? The answer resides in three glorious facts.

1. *As our High Priest, He Is Supremely Effective*

The author begins with a presupposition: 'Since then we have a great high priest who has passed through the heavens' (v. 14). The original recipients of this letter, Jewish by birth, would immediately recognize this as an assertion of Jesus' superior greatness over all other priests. On one day each year – Yom Kippur (the Day of Atonement) – the Levitical high priest departed from the sight of the people and carried the blood of atonement into the Holy of Holies. His journey inside took him through three portals. Firstly, he bore the blood into the Outer Court. Secondly, he crossed the threshold into the Holy Place. Thirdly, he passed through a veil into the Holy of Holies, the very presence of God Himself. Once inside, he would remain sufficiently long to sprinkle blood on the mercy seat atop the Ark of the Covenant, symbolically atoning for the sins of the people. Upon finishing, he would exit without delay. Tiny golden bells were sewn into the hem of his robe so that people outside could discern his movement. In the event the bells were silenced, they would recognize he had not survived the priestly experience.

Imagine the anxiety permeating this sacred drama. Certainly there must have been great angst on the part of the high priest. And what of the people outside – standing absolutely still, not daring to breathe, straining to hear the tinkling of the golden bells, wondering if the high priest would re-emerge? Yet all this meticulous ritual – and the breathless apprehension associated with it – never satisfactorily atoned for even the most insignificant of sins: a single white lie, a momentary bad attitude, a fleeting prideful thought.

For what reason, then, was this sacramental ceremony established? It served a prophetic function, foreshadowing the atonement offered by the ultimate priest: the sacrifice of His own life on the cross. But can we be certain that *this offering* was no mere religious ritual? That atonement was *actually* and *efficaciously* achieved? Yes – because God raised Him from the dead! Following forty days of post-resurrection ministry, He then departed from the sight of His followers, 'passing through the heavens' into the Most Holy Place, from which there was no urgency to exit, as implied by a verb tense that stresses ongoing results. Our great high priest has entered into the Holy of Holies – the very throne room of God – and *is still there*. Moreover, upon arriving He manifested the success of His accomplishment by an act that had never before been an expression of priestly ministry: He *sat down* – 'at the right hand of the Majesty on high' (Heb. 1:3). It was His exclamation mark to: 'It is finished.' This is a distinguishing feature of His superior greatness: He has accomplished what all other priests could only prefigure. As our high priest, He is supremely effective.

2. *As our High Priest, He Is Uniquely Qualified*

Who is this 'great high priest'? The author now reminds us of His identity: 'Jesus, the Son of God.' These words are much more than rhetorical embellishment. They seek to convey two qualities that distinguish this high priest from all others: 1) He is 'Jesus,' stressing His full *humanity*; and, 2) He is 'the Son of God,' stressing His full *deity*.

The qualification of a mediator turns on the basis

of his acceptability to the respective parties in need of reconciliation. As such, there could be no greater or more effective mediator between God and humanity than this priest. As deity, He can speak to God on equal terms. As human, He can represent us perfectly. Theologians refer to this dialectic more formally as 'the hypostatic union'– the fully divine/fully human natures united in the single person of Jesus Christ.

In all of Christian theology this is, without question, a doctrine that defies comprehensive penetration. Nevertheless, it is certainly possible to appreciate the emphasis here being made. This label of identification – 'Jesus, the Son of God' – draws together two truths the Hebrew writer has already labored to establish. In chapter one, he strongly accentuated the deity of the Son of God. In chapter two, he underscored the humanity of Jesus in equally ardent terms. Now, in the present text, he unites these truths in a mysterious convergence that in no way diminishes the uniqueness of each: Jesus (altogether human), the Son of God (altogether divine). As such, He is uniquely qualified to exercise a priestly mediation between the holy God and fallen humanity. He possesses a theanthropic stature that distinguishes Him as the ultimate priest. He is uniquely qualified.

3.   *As our High Priest, He Is Perfectly Compassionate*
Some of the Hebrew Christians, as they faced the reality of persecution, may have begun to question the extent to which Jesus could still identify with the cost of a worldly Christianity. 'Now that Jesus has entered the perfection

of glory at the Father's side, is He effectively insensible to the opposition we are enduring? Can He still, now in His majestic eminence, identify with our painful struggles and violent temptations?' The answer is: most certainly! Unparalleled understanding and compassion distinguish the superiority of our high priest. The Hebrew writer conveys this from a twofold perspective. *Negatively*, he writes: 'For we do not have a high priest who is unable to sympathize with our weaknesses.' *Positively*, he adds: 'but one who in every respect has been tempted as we are, yet without sin.' Clearly, our high priest's capacity to sympathize with human weakness is parallel to the fact that He has been tested in every way and to the fullest extent.

Because Jesus possessed a fully divine nature, many tend to believe He was ultimately impervious to temptation. But this is a heterodox view, in that it diminishes the *fullness* of His humanity. The apostle John strongly warns against this distortion:

> Beloved, do not believe every spirit, but test the spirits to see whether they are from God ... By this you know the Spirit of God: every spirit that confesses that Jesus Christ has come in the flesh is from God (1 John 4:1-2).

Paul declares Jesus 'born of woman, born under the law' (Gal. 4:4). Astoundingly, he writes that God sent His Son 'in the likeness of sinful flesh' (Rom. 8:3). Hebrews insists that Jesus shared in the same 'flesh and blood' as all humanity (Heb. 2:14). In the early portions of Luke we read that

Jesus bore in His body the distinguishing mark of the old covenant: circumcision (Luke 2:21). Luke later informs us that Jesus 'increased in wisdom and in stature' – that He developed intellectually and physically (Luke 2:52). Jesus encountered hunger (Luke 4:2). He endured weariness and thirst (John 4:6-7). He felt sorrow (Matt. 26:37-38). He experienced death (John 19:30). Moreover, His side was pierced to verify death, and the consequence was the necessary evidence of blood and water (John 19:34). It is striking that the very first reference to the coming of Jesus says nothing regarding His deity. We are only informed that He would be the *offspring of Eve*: 'I will put enmity between you and the woman, and between your offspring and her offspring; he shall bruise your head, and you shall bruise his heel' (Gen. 3:15). In fact, that the serpent would bruise His heel displays vulnerability does it not – a distinctly *human* trait?

Jesus Christ was no superhuman. He was human as we are human. He possessed an authentically human body, mind, and emotions, bearing all the inherent weaknesses and limitations associated with being human. Of course, we must equally affirm the deity of Jesus Christ – that He was certainly more than a man. But never was He less than a man. He entered this world as a man. He lived His life as a man. Every challenge He faced, He did so as a man. He is the ultimate human and the epitome of humanity. And it is precisely because of this that He can now express perfect compassion to His needy people.

Imagine yourself in a room with two pianos. Were you to strike middle C on one piano, the very same note on the other would also respond, even though you never touched it. *The Oxford Companion To Music* refers to this phenomenon as 'sympathetic resonance.' Similarly, Jesus' human instrument was identical to yours. By virtue of His resurrection, He has taken this same instrument to heaven so that even now, when a note is struck in the weakness of your human instrument it resonates in His.[1]

It is the fullness of Jesus' humanity that determines the extent to which He can presently sympathize with human weakness. Even more poignant is that, as a man, He was the object of every kind of temptation ('one who in every respect has been tempted as we are'). This is not to suggest that Jesus encountered *every* temptation. He was never tempted to watch too much television. He was never tempted to waste time surfing the Net. Nor did He ever face temptations unique to the elderly. Rather, Jesus experienced temptation in every area inherent to human weakness: pride, selfishness, revenge, greed, lust, doubt, fear. Distinguishing Him from every other priest, however, is the fact He never once surrendered to these temptations ('yet without sin').

All of this implies that Jesus endured temptation to a degree never experienced by any other human being. On what basis may this be legitimately assumed? The only way to endure the full force of temptation's power is to never yield. But every human being, minus Jesus, has yielded – and in so doing abbreviated his or her experience of

1. I am indebted to R. Kent Hughes for this helpful analogy.

temptation's full power. Jesus is the only sinless human being. And it is this sinlessness that reveals His exposure to the greatest possible intensity of temptation's power. Jesus endured all there is to endure – temptation to the 'nth' degree. This we know because He never yielded.

Are you familiar with Homer's legend of Odysseus? Returning victorious from the Trojan War, Odysseus finds it necessary to sail in close proximity to the island of the sirens – creatures that sing melodies of indescribable beauty. He is warned that no man can resist the allure of their vocalizing, and that all who yield are summarily killed on the shore of their island. Accordingly, Odysseus orders his men to stop their ears with wax. But they are also instructed to fasten him to the ship's mast with his ears left unstopped. If he attempts to free himself they are to bind him more tightly. When Odysseus finally comes within the sound of the sirens' voices, powerful longings begin to surge within so that he is in an agony of desire to succumb. Nevertheless, as he struggles to free himself, his deaf sailors truss him more forcefully. He experiences the fullest intensity of the sirens' temptation while simultaneously powerless to do what was bade him – lashed, as he was, to the crossbeam of the mast.

Jesus had no men to whom He could give such orders. Yet, throughout the entirety of His life, the siren sought to lure Him away from the divine plan. Its appealing melody was heard in the wilderness: 'I will give you all the kingdoms of the world, if you will fall down and worship me.' Peter sang its tempting tones: 'The cross is no place for you, Lord!' It echoed again in the garden as Jesus pleaded with His Father: 'Must I drink from this cup?' But the siren's song was never more alluring than when, hanging on the cross, Jesus heard the lyric of the mob: 'If you are the Son of God, then come down from the cross.' It was the last great temptation of the siren – real and powerful – the intensity of its wickedness far greater than any temptation before or after. For the duration of His life the enemy sang it into His ears. It was the song that never ended. But Jesus never yielded. He remained faithful to the very end, because He had lashed Himself to the crossbeam of obedience.

Christians will occasionally debate the 'peccability' or 'impeccability' of Jesus Christ. It is a theological issue that seeks to answer the questions: 'Could Jesus sin? Was He merely *temptable*? Or was He truly *susceptible*?' All Christians agree that Jesus *did not* sin. But the question still stands: *Could* He have sinned? Some say *no*, others *yes*. Despite the different conclusions – typically the consequence of rational deductions – Christians on both sides of the issue must at least acknowledge the clear record of the sacred text: the sinlessness of Jesus is always pictured as a result of conscious decision and intense struggle rather than as a formal consequence of His deity.

This is why there is now sympathetic resonance in heaven. He is a high priest who is perfectly compassionate because, *as a man*, He Himself has endured the fullness of temptation's power.

> Therefore he had to be made like his brothers in every respect, so that he might become a merciful and faithful high priest in the service of God, to make propitiation for the sins of the people. For because he himself has suffered when tempted, he is able to help those who are being tempted (Heb 2:17-18).

There is no temptation we endure with which He cannot identify – *He has been tempted in every respect*. There is no temptation we endure that exceeds His capacity to help – *He has never yielded*. This distinguishes His superior greatness as our high priest.

At this point one would do well to remember that the wider context of this section concerns the subject of perseverance – enduring in faithfulness to the gospel. Now the writer displays an essential element to this theme: 'Let us then with confidence draw near to the throne of grace' (v. 16a).

The perfect sacrifice of Jesus has been accepted, and its consequence made exceedingly obvious by a graphic incident: the rending from top to bottom of the veil leading into the Holy of Holies. As such, Christians now have access into the very presence chamber of God. While a 'throne' is still present – reminding us of God's unchanging sovereignty – it is, by virtue of the accomplishments of our great high priest, now defined as 'the throne of grace.' From this gracious throne two commodities will need to be repeatedly acquired. Firstly, there is 'mercy' to be received. But what does this presuppose: that our expressions of perseverance will be less-than-perfect; that an inconsistency will mark the most faithful Christian. Here there is no cheap triumphalism, over-realized eschatology, or entire sanctification – not this side of the new creation. When we do fall, however, and return to our Father in brokenness, we will find mercy rather than condemnation because sitting at His right hand is our high priest bearing the evidence of His redemptive accomplishments.

> My little children, I am writing these things to you so that you may not sin. But if anyone does sin, we have an advocate with the Father, Jesus Christ the righteous. He is the propitiation for our sins, and not for ours only but also for the sins of the whole world (1 John 2:1-2).

The second commodity to be acquired at this throne is 'grace.' It is available for help 'in time of need' – at the moment we require it. An authentic Christianity that is meaningfully worldly will demand a stubborn perseverance. Divinely supplied grace will prove essential as a means of steadily deepening one's faithfulness to Jesus through the various oppositions we encounter. It will be necessary for the courage to advance the gospel despite the multitude of fears – both real and imagined – that plague us. Grace must be sought as a recurring provision if we are to endure to the end and fulfill our charge in this world.

But how easily accessible are 'mercy' and 'grace'? Under the old covenant, *one man* entered the Holy of Holies. Moreover, his entrance into that place was confined to *once a year*. Here a wonderful contrast is illustrated – in part, by a vast broadening of the *scope* of people who may enter

God's presence: 'Let *us*,' those of us who have Jesus Christ as our high priest. *All of us* are summoned to this 'throne of grace.' The contrast is illustrated further by a limitless increase in the *frequency* with which we may draw near to God's throne. The durative sense of the original text should be read as follows: 'Let us *keep on continually drawing near* to the throne of grace.' This assures us that we will never exhaust God or drain our allotment of His mercy and grace. We are summoned to persistently draw near.

This is how a worldly Christian perseveres: regularly coming before the Father in prayer, seeking His mercy for failures and His grace for enduring faithfulness. And why are we told to do so 'with confidence'? There is a priest in God's presence who has felt the full force of temptation's power and who, because He never sinned, knows exactly what we need at the moment we need it.

> There is a man, a real man,
> With wounds still gaping wide,
> From which rich streams of blood once ran
> In hands, and feet and side.
> 'Tis no wild fancy of our minds,
> No metaphor we make;
> The same dear man in heaven now reigns,
> Who suffered for our sake.
>
> This wondrous man of whom we tell
> Is true almighty God;
> He bought our souls from death and hell;

The price His own heart's blood.
That human heart He still retains,
Though throned in highest bliss,
And feels each tempted member's pains,
Our own afflictions His.

Come, then, repenting sinner, come,
Approach with humble faith,
Whate'er you owe, the total sum
Is cancelled by His death.
His blood can cleanse the blackest soul
And wash our guilt away;
He will present us sound and whole
On that tremendous day
(Joseph Hart 1712–1768).

For we do not have a high priest who is unable to sympathize with our weaknesses, but one who in every respect has been tempted as we are, yet without sin. Let us then with confidence draw near to the throne of grace, that we may receive mercy and find grace to help in time of need (Heb. 4:15-16).

It is the only way to persevere as a worldly Christian.

Spirit Empowered Preaching

Involving the Holy Spirit in Your Ministry

ARTURO G. AZURDIA III

One of the great dangers that faces today's preachers is the problem of an over-intellectual approach. Careful, meditative and painstaking exegesis brings a potential liability, that of losing the vitality which must accompany exposition.

The Puritans called it 'that certain unction', Martyn Lloyd-Jones called it 'an access of power', others have called it 'the anointing'. If you desire that your preaching be lifted up to a position in which you are being used by the Spirit as a channel, then Arturo Azurdia can help you.

> 'If your praying for the Spirit's power has become formal or thoughtless then this book can change both you and your ministry – by the Spirit's power.'
>
> Edmund P. Clowney

> 'When you finish reading this book not only will you have a better idea of the role of the Spirit in preaching, but you will also know better how to preach in dependence on the Holy Spirit. Everyone who is preaching, or preparing to preach, needs to read this book'
>
> Joey Pipa

> 'Arturo Azurdia believes that much modern preaching is powerless. Sadly, he is right ... in a searching and warm-hearted analysis he shows how the situation should and can be remedied.'
>
> John Blanchard

ISBN 978-1-85792-413-8

Also available related to Christian life in the world ...

CONCISE PORTABLE SPIRITUAL FOOD · MATTHEW

UNDERSTANDING
THE TIMES

LIVING IN THE LIGHT OF THE ARRIVAL OF THE KING

WILLIAM TAYLOR

Understanding the Times

Living in the Light of the Arrival of the King

WILLIAM TAYLOR

How should churches and individual Christians react to the increasingly secular and amoral world in which we live? Through a study of three key chapters in Matthew's Gospel (ch. 8-10), Taylor argues that Matthew wanted his readers to understand God's perspective on the times in which we live. Through an analysis of the way in which Matthew presents the miracles Jesus performed and the teaching He gave His disciples, Taylor concludes that we do not live in a day which calls for judgment and condemnation, but rather one demanding gut-wrenching compassion for sinners and a bold proclamation of the forgiveness of sins Jesus came to bring. The arrival of King Jesus inaugurated the era of His kingdom rule, a foretaste of the world to come, but we still live in a fallen world, which will inevitably be in conflict with His kingdom people. Taylor draws out the lessons Matthew was teaching about the terms and conditions of discipleship and the family ties of kingdom living. Above all, the urgent need for persevering and intense prayer is emphasized.

This book contains questions for further study at the end of each chapter, making it useful for both individual and group study. There are also helpful comments for those wishing to preach on these chapters.

ISBN 978-1-84550-438-0

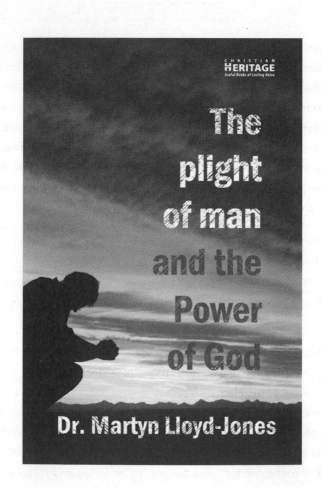

The Plight of Man and the Power of God
DR MARTYN LLOYD-JONES

Martyn Lloyd-Jones's preaching always had an emphasis on the desperate plight of man and the power of God to save. His preaching was crystal clear on the sovereignty of God in the salvation of sinners, a concept that does not sit comfortably in our day of pragmatism, programs and self-help books. Nevertheless it remains at the core of what the world needs to hear. Based on the Romans 1, this wonderful book will help you understand what the gospel is. When we live in a world that is spiralling out of control we will want to hear this message again and again.

> We must rouse ourselves and realize afresh that though our Gospel is timeless and changeless, it nevertheless is always contemporary. We must meet the present situation and we must speak a word to the world that none else can speak.
>
> Dr Martyn Lloyd-Jones

Dr. Martyn Lloyd-Jones (1899-1981) was born in Wales. At the age of 27 he gave up a most promising medical career to become a preacher... When a spiritual history of the 20th century comes to be written it will be bound to include mention not only the far-reaching influence of Dr. Lloyd-Jones' ministry at Westminster Chapel in London, England from 1938-68, but of the remarkable fact that his published volumes of expository sermons have had an unprecedented circulation for such material, selling in millions of copies.

ISBN 978-1-84550-439-9

'This book fills a long-awaited need. It makes the Proverbs accessible... a rich resource for every reader.' JOHN MACARTHUR

PRACTICING PROVERBS

WISE LIVING FOR FOOLISH TIMES

RICHARD MAYHUE

Practicing Proverbs
Wise Living for Foolish Times

RICHARD MAYHUE

This is a unique book on a unique part of Scripture. Mayhue introduces us to Solomon, the writer of Proverbs, and then gets to grips with the book itself and its message. He answers some of the most frequently asked questions about Proverbs and how the book has immediate and pressing relevance to Christians today.

Then he reorganizes the text of the entire book of Proverbs into six life applications – spiritual, personal, family, intellectual, market-place and societal – each also having particular themes highlighted within them.

Practicing Proverbs is one book with multiple uses: devotional, small group discipleship book, resource for the biblical counselor and for teaching Christian ethics and morality.

Most importantly of all, this is a book to help the reader develop a life that glorifies the source of all wisdom – God.

> *Practicing Proverbs* is one of the most practical books you will ever read! Why? Because Richard Mayhue bases his thoughts and unique arrangement of materials on one of the most helpful books of the Bible. Ever since Mayhue's conversion he has incorporated these same principles into his daily life, and with tremendous effect. You too can experience the same great blessing in your life. I would strongly encourage everyone to read this book!
>
> Dr. Tim LaHaye
> Author, Minister, Educator

ISBN 978-1-85792-777-1

Christian Focus Publications

publishes books for all ages
Our mission statement -

STAYING FAITHFUL

In dependence upon God we seek to impact the world through literature faithful to his infallible word, the Bible. Our aim is to ensure that the Lord Jesus Christ is presented as the only hope to obtain forgiveness of sin, live a useful life and look forward to heaven with Him.

REACHING OUT

Christ's last command requires us to reach out to our world with His gospel. We seek to help fulfil that by publishing books that point people towards Jesus and help them develop a Christ-like maturity. We aim to equip all levels of readers for life, work, ministry and mission.

Books in our adult range are published in three imprints:

Christian Focus contains popular works including biographies, commentaries, basic doctrine and Christian living. Our children's books are also published in this imprint.

Mentor focuses on books written at a level suitable for Bible College and seminary students, pastors, and other serious readers. The imprint includes commentaries, doctrinal studies, examination of current issues and church history.

Christian Heritage contains classic writings from the past.

Christian Focus Publications Ltd
Geanies House, Fearn, Ross-shire,
IV20 1TW, Scotland, United Kingdom.
info@christianfocus.com
www.christianfocus.com